RISE, PRAY

& SLAY:

STRATEGIES TO HEAL THE LAND

LINDA D. LEE, PCLC, CCM

Award-winning author

LL Media Group LLC
Where Freedom Reigns

Scripture quotations marked (NKJV) are taken from the Holman Study Bible NKJV Edition, Copyright © 2013. Used by the permission of Holman Bible Publishers, Inc., Nashville, Tennessee. All other scriptures are indicated by their different translations. All rights reserved.

DEFINITIONS

Let's begin with some important definitions!

Rise, /rīz/, *verb*

1. move from a lower position to a higher one; come or go up. 2. Get up from lying, sitting, or kneeling.
synonyms: stand up, get/**rise** to one's feet, **get up**.

Pray, /prā/, *verb*

1. address a solemn request or expression of thanks to a deity or other object of worship.
synonyms: say one's prayers, be at prayer, make one's **devotions**; offer a prayer/prayers, commune with "let us pray" invoke, call on, implore, appeal to, entreat, beseech, beg, ask/**request earnestly**.

Slay, /slā/, *verb*

1. ARCHAIC•LITERARY
kill (a person or animal) in a violent way.
synonyms: kill, murder, put to death, do to death, put to the sword, butcher, cut to pieces, **slaughter**, massacre, shoot down, gun down, assassinate, execute, **destroy**, eliminate, **annihilate**, exterminate, dispose of.

The online dictionary provides these definitions. Use them to understand why a prayer regimen is important to build a healthy work culture for this generation and the next.

Acknowledgment

"Prayer is not an activity, and it is not an application. It is life found in a person. Once you see Jesus, once the blinders fall away from your eyes in the glory of His presence, your attitudes about prayer will totally change! This thing of prayer, this thing of intercession, of standing in the gap, of making an appeal to a superior – it is not a hard task! It is a joy. It's called life in the Kingdom."- James W. Goll[1]

LINDA D. LEE

Table of Content

LINDA D. LEE

Introduction

"In the United States, school prayer cannot be required of students in accordance with the establishment clause of the First Amendment to the United States Constitution the legal basis for this prohibition is the First Amendment to the United States Constitution, which requires that, 'Congress shall make no law respecting an establishment of religion, or prohibiting the free exercise thereof...' The First Amendment (Amendment 1) to the United States Constitution prevents the government from making laws which respect an establishment of religion, prohibit the free exercise, of religion, or abridge the freedom of speech, the freedom of the press, the right to peaceably assemble, or the right to petition the government for redress of grievance. It was adopted on Dec. 15, 1791, as one of the ten amendments that constitute the Bill of Rights." [2]

How ironic is it that in 1960 the late Madalyn

Murray O'Hair, atheist, social worker, and civil rights activist, filed the landmark lawsuit against forcing her son to participate in Bible reading while attending public school? Although she won her court case, many people suffered from the trauma behind the entire ordeal. Her action shifted the world regarding an active prayer life. Especially, when it related to children praying in school. However, the debate between separation of church and state continues. A plain-text reading of the Amendment says, "'no law shall be made to impede free exercise of religion." So, they say "separation of church and state." I say <u>there</u> <u>would</u> <u>be</u> <u>no</u> <u>state</u> <u>without</u> <u>the</u> <u>church</u>.[3] And the cohort from this anthology agrees!

They took prayer out of everything. And, we're putting it back in!

Millions of global influencers, entrepreneurs, Kingdompreneurs, and thought-leaders have been searching for sustainability strategies to grow their business. One strategy, prayer, has been hidden in plain sight for centuries. In *Rise, Pray & Slay: Strategies to Heal the Land*, we expose the truth about "separation of church and state" through the transformation stories of seven phenomenal overcomers. Most importantly, you'll develop a prayer regimen to shift your workplace culture while changing your mindset. Furthermore, you will learn how to *Rise, Pray & Slay* anything that tries to block or hinder your success!

It is time for the church to take a stand! Especially, with the current state of America. More and more Christians are being told their religious beliefs or prayer has no place in schools or in the workplace. Or should I say, society has accepted a watered-down restriction to prayer in schools, and simultaneously, very little prayer in the workplace. It is time to change this mindset.

Recently, I read a story out of Washington D.C. entitled, "Holistic Approach Needed to Change

Workplace Culture to Prevent Harassment, Experts Tell EEOC." Then it hit me. If we need a holistic approach in the workplace to prevent harassment, we also need a holistic approach to everything else. Especially, in the workplace, where there has been numerous reported mass shooting and active shooter cases globally.

Today, we want to answer the call-to-action by offering seven holistic strategies from phenomenal overcomers that will shift the culture (atmosphere) around you. Washington D.C. recognized what many people have been saying for years: "A holistic approach is needed to change the workplace culture." It is time for us to reintroduce some strategies to assist them and you in *Rise, Pray & Slay: Strategies to Heal the Land.* Now, no matter whether you are at work, church, a business meeting, Mastermind, summit, workshop, seminar, or teleconference, you can feel comfortable stealing-away to pray like these phenomenal overcomers. Get ready to learn prayers, strategies, phenomenal prayer tools, and much more so you can *Rise, Pray & Slay* in life, business, or career to heal the land!

CHAPTER 2

Renew Your Mind!

By Dr. Lindie Sanders

Some people rise and seek God early, while others wait till something drastic happens.

I was taught that education was the key to success. So, I prayed for and got my first scholarship at age 20 while facing a bad marriage. When I told my mother about the scholarship opportunity, she quietly said, "Take the scholarship. Education is the husband that will never let you down." I took the scholarship and left Mozambique for Ohio where I completed a two-year certificate. That triggered a desire to pursue higher education and, throughout the next 15 years, I earned two scholarships to continue my studies in Arizona while raising a family.

Throughout my college education, I acquired knowledge of my craft. I handled my busy life well, so I thought. I failed to realize that I lacked wisdom to understand that God, the giver of knowledge, deserved my attention sometime during my busy day. I used to pull all-nighters studying and waking up just in time to get dressed, get the kids to school, and navigate through rush hour to get to work in the morning, school in the evening and then home to get some rest and do it all over again the next day.

In the Fall of 1995, a string of misfortunes hit my family. My younger brother died in a car crash in South Africa in his early thirties, leaving two very little girls. All of a sudden, friends were coming in and out of my home to pray and offer words of comfort. I wasn't comforted; I needed answers from God as to why our lives were abruptly turned upside down. I couldn't wait for an answer because I had three weeks to fly to Johannesburg, South Africa, bury my brother and come back to work. When I realized that I couldn't bring my little nieces with me because of visa restrictions, my pain worsened. However, I couldn't deal with the pain because I needed to make arrangements with family members to take care of my brother's babies.

Once I got back on my feet, I turned to God and prayed before starting my day. A void needed to be filled. God answered my question and told me that we had not invited Him into our busy lives. I repented. Since then, He has been filling my cup with joy and peace daily no matter what the day brings.

It is time to Rise, Pray & Slay!

Co-author reflection on the scripture:

"I needed that <u>hiding place</u> to survive and <u>renew</u> my carnal mind. I find that each time I'm in a survival mode, I go back to that <u>place</u> <u>of</u> <u>safety</u> and renew my mind."

- Dr. Lindie Sanders

Colossians 3:2-3 (NKJV)
New King James Version

"Set your mind on things above, not on things on the earth. For you died, and your life is hidden with Christ in God."

Phenomenal Prayer Strategy:

A. Find your secret place to pray (not necessarily a physical place).
B. Renew your mind and strength.
C. Focus on your assignment, vision or mission.
D. Surround yourself with a solid support System.

Renew Your Mind!
Exercise

One of the main excuses people have for not praying is, "I don't have enough time." Annotate any excuse you have for not making prayer a priority in your life, business or career to renew your mind.

1.
_____
2.
_____
3.
_____
4.
_____
5.
_____
6.
_____
7.
_____
8.
_____
9.
_____
10.
_____

Lord, renew my mind and remove my excuses!

SAMPLE PRAYER

Prayer time: _____ AM or _____ PM

Prayer day(s): _____

Beginning Each Day

"Father, today belongs to You! I will celebrate and be glad wherever I may be. It is better to obey than to sacrifice, so I submit to Your will so that my plans and purposes may be conducted in a manner that will bring honor and glory to You. Thank You for keeping me spiritually and mentally alert in this time of meditation and prayer.

I completely trust You and place myself and those for whom I pray in your keeping, while knowing You are able to guard everything and everyone that I entrust to You. Thank You for ordering Your angels to protect me, my family and my friends. They will hold us up with their hands so that we won't even hurt our feet on a stone. Thank You, Father that Your love never ends and Your mercy never stops. Your loyalty to me is awesome!

Father, I kneel in prayer to You. You are wonderful and glorious. I pray that Your Spirit will make me a strong follower and that Christ will live in the heart because of my faith.

You can do anything, Father—far more than I could ever imagine or guess or request in my wildest dreams by Your Spirit within me. Glory to Your forever! Amen."[5] Now let's gain an understanding of "separation between church and state."

It is time to Rise, Pray & Slay!

Prayer Never Fails

In the mist of penning *Rise, Pray & Slay: Strategies to Heal the Land*, I ran across a passionate movie in the faith section of our TV channel called *Prayer Never Fails,* directed by Wes Miller. First, the title captivated me as revelation started coming forth after reading the movie synopsis: "When a high-school basketball coach is fired for praying with a player, he teams up with a not-so-saintly lawyer to take his fight to the courts."

You know I have to share a few nuggets from this POWERFUL movie. In this semi-intense movie, every scene was riddled with divine revelation of a continuous walk of faith by all the main characters. The basketball coach routinely prayed with his boys, as he called them, after each practice. It was in his DNA to automatically pray and he wanted to groom the players to become men. He was surprisingly thrown-for-a-loop one evening when one of his players came to him for help. The player hinted that he was a victim of paternal abuse. Unfortunately, the accused abuser was the town's judge. He seemed like a mean, arrogant alpha male high on a dose of pride. Do you know anyone that wants to accuse "a judge" of abusing their child? Not me.

Well, to make a long story short, the player didn't want to "say" his father had beaten him. Instead, he asked the coach, "What would he do?" As expected, the coach recommended the player pray. But he didn't know how to pray. He wanted the coach to pray for him. Now picture the scene changing, as two witnesses see both of them in a classroom with the coach praying for his player. By the time this news reaches the principal and the player's father, the coach had already jeopardized losing his job. Everyone involved was aware of the school policy prohibiting the coach from praying with his players. And, it wasn't that the coach did not care about the school policy. Simply, he wanted others to respect "his right" to pray under the First Amendment to the Constitution. After a heated meeting with the principal, judge, and his player, the coach was unjustly terminated. In a short period of time, he started feeling defeated when no would hire him. It was only after his basketball team showed up at his home to remind him of some affirmations and wisdom which he had shared with them as encouragement. He always instilled in them to "fight" for what they knew was right. Unfortunately, feeling of defeat begun to grip him. He was losing his will to fight and stand for what he knew was right. Have you ever felt like that? I have.

You do know he "came to himself," like the prodigal son.

Afterwards, he later hired an attorney to fight for his reinstatement based on his First Amendment right to free speech and "separation of church and state." The coach felt he had the "right" to pray for his player or anyone else at any appointed time.

We hear people mention "separation of church and state," but what actually does that mean?

"The phrase "separation between church and state" is generally traced to a January 1, 1802, letter by Thomas Jefferson, addressed to the Danbury Baptist Association in Connecticut, and published in a Massachusetts newspaper. Jefferson wrote, "**Believing**

with you that religion is a matter which lies solely between Man & his God that he owes account to none other for his faith or his worship, that the legitimate powers of government reach actions only, & not opinions I contemplate with sovereign reverence that act of the whole American people which declared that their legislature should **'make no law respecting an establishment of religion, or prohibiting the free exercise thereof,' thus building a wall of separation between Church & State.** Adhering to this expression of the supreme will of the nation in behalf of the rights of conscience I shall see with sincere satisfaction the progress of those sentiments which tend to **restore to man all his natural rights,** convinced he has no natural right in opposition to his social duties."[6] Awesome!

Contrary to what you see and hear in the world today, you have the right outwardly and inwardly to *Rise, Pray & Slay* everywhere you go! Yes, there may be departmental policies and global restrictions that limit you from expressing your religious beliefs or praying. However, those polices cannot hinder you from exercising the strategies in *Rise, Pray & Slay: Strategies to Heal the Land* to change the culture of your workplace. The atmosphere of many workplaces has become contaminated with a lot of foolishness, as Satan has been given a foothold to enter it. Again, prayer never fails! You need a prayer life, prayer regimen, intercessors, prayer call, prayer warriors, spiritual warfare prayers, prayers of comfort, health and healing prayers, and much more BEFORE you even arrive to your work.

Never allow the issue of separation between church and state to prevent you from exercising your right to *Rise, Pray & Slay!* Implement these strategies and see what happens.

It is time to Rise, Pray & Slay!

CHAPTER 3

The Faces of Depression

By Debbie Humphrey

For many years my mind was clogged with a myth that mental illness was restricted or attached to a certain race, color, or creed of people. Depression is certainly a silent killer that speaks loud and clear to all who suffer with its seasons in or out of the body of Christ. Depression has a face that looks like mine and yours.

The death of Robin Williams shocked many of us, but yet it was real to me. Many of us didn't know his battle with depression. Robin hid behind making others laugh so they wouldn't see his pain. Let's make this thing relatable! Depression became real when the face became mine. My face was always on point, my hair was something to reckon with, and I dressed and carried some of the finest things. Church was routine and living for Him was a lifestyle I chose. Depression became something I adorned myself with it, and it was like a string of pearls that I would lay to dress my garment daily! Depression has a beautiful face, but a broken soul, and it has a flawless fit, but yet is fearful! It's camouflaged on the face of the very elite. The face of depression can only hide its identity to those who've never been there—I lived to tell the story.

I WAS the face of depression!

I had to identify it to rise above it! I had to own it to slay it! When I identified and owned this place, I learned to pray myself out of the deep place. As God begins to reveal your issue, you must call the issue by its name to get a response or get someone's attention! When I called depression by its name, it quickly started to loosen its hold. However, it wasn't an easy fight! Being a church girl exempted me from this fight, so I thought, but it actually qualified me with the tools to help others. Revelations 12:11 states, "And they overcame him by the blood of the Lamb and by the word of their testimony, and they did not love their lives to the death."

Co-author reflection on the scripture:

"The more I spoke about my struggle the lighter I felt. My eyes became clear. My peace returned one day at a time."

-Debbie Humphrey

Phenomenal Prayer Strategy:

John 9: 4-5
New International Version (NIV)

"As long as it is day, we must do the works of him who sent me. Night is coming, when no one can work. While I am in the world, I am the light of the world."

Be open, honest and transparent when communicating with God in private or in public.

The Faces of Depression

Red Flags

❖ Mood: anxiety, apathy, general discontent, guilt, hopelessness, loss of interest or pleasure in activities, mood swings, or sadness.

❖ Sleep: early awakening, excess sleepiness, insomnia, or restless sleep.

❖ Whole body: excessive hunger, fatigue, loss of appetite or restlessness.

❖ Behavioral: agitation, excessive crying, irritability, or social isolation.

❖ Cognitive: lack of concentration slowness in activity, or thoughts of suicide.

❖ Weight: weight gain or weight loss.

❖ Also common: poor appetite or repeatedly going over thought.

❖ More.

Source: Mayo Clinic

The Faces of Depression Exercise

Depression looks different to many people. Identify areas in your life where darkness seems to reside (for example, life, business, career, etc.).

1. _____

2. _____

3. _____

4. _____

5. _____

6. _____

7. _____

8. _____

9. _____

10. _____

Lord, remove the <u>root</u> of depression from my life!

SAMPLE PRAYER

Prayer time: _____ AM or _____ PM

Prayer day(s): _____

Victory Over Depression

"Father, You are my shelter and my refuge in times of trouble, even here in the midst of depression. Regardless of these negative feelings I choose to lean on and put my trust in You, for You will not abandon me. I put my hope in You and praise You, my Savior and my God. Depression is an enemy and has no place here!

Lord, You lift me up when I am weighed down and protect me when I allow feelings of anxiety. So, I purpose to wait on You, Lord, and when I feel weak, the Holy Spirit reminds me to say that I am strong. With Your help, my heart takes courage. You are saving me and helping me establish myself in rightness—in conformity with Your will and order. I resist the feelings of depression and declare I am far from even the thought of oppression or destruction; I am not afraid and terror cannot come near me. I trust in the name of Jesus, and I rely on You, Lord.

Father, You have thoughts and plans for my welfare and peace, to give me a future and a hope. When my thoughts are fixed on You, You keep me in perfect peace. Peace of mind and heart I receive from You as a gift so I will not be troubled or afraid.

In the name of Jesus, I loose self-defeating thought patterns from my mind. I tear down strongholds that have protected bad perceptions about myself. I give myself completely to You, Father and take my stand against fear, discouragement, self-pity and depression. I will not give the devil a way to defeat me by harboring resentment, holding onto self-hatred, anger toward myself and others or feeling guilty. I surround myself with songs and shouts of deliverance from depression, and I will continue to gain the victory by the blood of Jesus and the word of my witness.

Father, I receive a spirit of power, love, and a calm and well-balanced mind with discipline and self-control, which You have given me. I cooperate with the Spirit of God who is helping me renew my thoughts and attitudes with Your Word. Thank You for giving me Christ's way of thinking so I can now make intelligent decisions without fear.

You are the Lifter of the head, and I walk a straight path-healed and whole. I arise from the depression and circumstances that have kept me down. I rise to new life; I shine with the glory of the Lord.

You have rescued me from this evil world in which I live and I praise You, for the joy of the Lord is my strength. Amen."[5]

It is time to Rise, Pray & Slay!

CHAPTER 4

Defeating Abandonment Disguised as Love

By Sha-Miracle Demus

As I think of my journey, I am reminded of the many trials that were perfectly purposed to position me into my place of destiny. The journey although filled with tumultuous twists and turns, has taught me to persevere through the pain with poise. God's grace has embellished my story with strength, courage and resilience, and for that I am grateful and blessed. The pressure applied to my life has been immensely intense, yet with God I have been able to OVERCOME the trauma of toxic relationships that were sent to destroy and prevent the call on my life. Each relationship that I experienced released a poisonous secretion of abandonment, deceit, manipulation, emotional abuse, and betrayal that caused me to question my existence and overall sense of value and self-worth not only as a woman but as a human being. The trauma that I endured triggered my growth in God, expanded my faith, strengthened my prayers, and taught me to slaughter the spirit of abandonment that was hoovering dangerously over my life.

I appeared to be the "IT GIRL." I was perceived as the one who was confident, happy and self-assured. However, the truth was that I was desperately struggling to love myself and accept the fact that I was severely broken by the controlling ways and ill intentions of men. They preyed on my innocence, my faithfulness and my inexperience. Therefore, I found myself entangled in a web of lies and infidelity. The scars ran deep and devastated me to the point of wanting to take my life. The spirit of suicide began to saturate my mind. It wanted me to believe that I could never recover from the abuse and the hurt. Nor did it want me to believe that I was capable of being loved the way God intended me to be or move forward in healing.

The process I endured involved God purging me from the poison of these relationships by allowing me to own my responsibility in making decisions that did not honor him. The Lord has been faithful in repairing me through his forgiveness, righteousness and unfailing love.

Co-author reflection on the scripture

"That scripture is significant to my testimony as <u>God</u> has <u>allowed</u> me to <u>rise above</u> what was meant to <u>ruin me</u> through the

Acts 26:16
New International Version (NIV)

"Now get up and stand on your feet. I have appeared to you to appoint you as a servant and as a witness of what you have seen and will see of me."

string of toxic relationships that I endured. God showed me the meaning of his grace so that I could share his revelation and his love."

-Sha-Miracle Demus

Phenomenal Prayer Strategy:

Focus on GOD and not the issues meant to destroy you in any relationship.

It is time to Rise, Pray & Slay!

Defeating Abandonment Exercise

Abandonment is a root cause to a lot of dysfunctional relationships today. Annotate any toxic relationship or experience still hurting you.

1. _____

2. _____

3. _____

4. _____

5. _____

6. _____

7. _____

8. _____

9. _____

10. _____

Lord, remove my desire for these relationships, immediately!

SAMPLE PRAYER

Prayer time: _____ AM or _____ PM

Prayer day(s): _____

Overcoming the Feeling of Abandonment

"Father, I have confessed Jesus as my Lord, and I believe in my heart that you raised Him from the dead. I ask you Holy Spirit to help me overcome the resentment I feel toward those who abused and abandoned me. Now I am your child. When other people leave me and I feel unloved, I am thankful that you have promise that you will never leave nor fail me or abandoned me. Jesus you gave your life for me and called me a friend. You live in my heart and I am on my way to heaven. I have so much to be thankful for, and I do as your word says and be thankful in all circumstances. So, when I am lonely or discouraged, I will think of things that are true and honest and right. Heavenly father, I ask you to make me strong—I ask you to make me strong and help me while dangers surrounds me. You have ordered your angels to guard over me. I am not alone. Your word says that nothing can ever separate me from your love, not even my fears for today or worries about tomorrow. I will come to the top of every circumstance or trial through God's love. Lord, you are concerned with the smallest details of my life. You will work out your plans for my life and I can trust you because you are already, you are ready to help when I need you. Lord, I need you at all times. Lord, I ask you for true friends. Tell me how to trust others, be friends, and be a friend who sticks by like a God-fearing family helped me to walk in your love and show myself friendly."[5]

It is time to Rise, Pray & Slay!

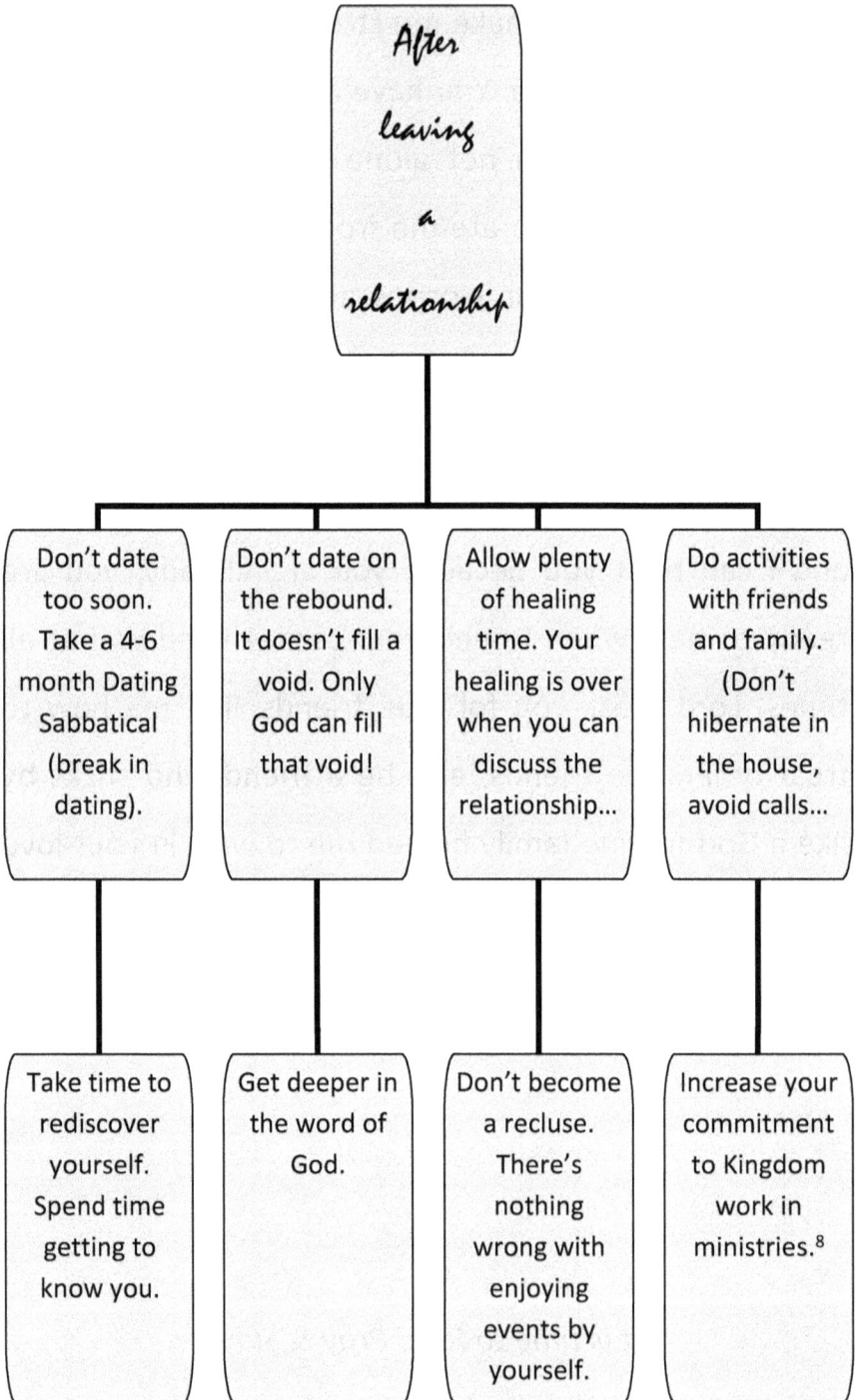

After

leaving

a

relationship

| Don't date too soon. Take a 4-6 month Dating Sabbatical (break in dating). | Don't date on the rebound. It doesn't fill a void. Only God can fill that void! | Allow plenty of healing time. Your healing is over when you can discuss the relationship... | Do activities with friends and family. (Don't hibernate in the house, avoid calls... |

| Take time to rediscover yourself. Spend time getting to know you. | Get deeper in the word of God. | Don't become a recluse. There's nothing wrong with enjoying events by yourself. | Increase your commitment to Kingdom work in ministries.[8] |

Hiding in Plain Sight

What do you do when you have prayed, showed yourself friendly, and the unimaginable happens? The movie trailer says, "What would you do if you lost everything? The answer is a grim reality for Darrius and Josie Blackmun. A hardworking couple plagued by bad luck and tough circumstances, they watched their middle-class lifestyle crumble away as unemployment took his brutal toll. Now they have no shelter for their two children. They become homeless and they're living on the streets." I was introduced to this movie while on a speaking engagement for the former Black Women's Initiative (BWI) organization, under former president, Barack Obama. Director M. Legend Brown was at this event sharing bits and pieces of his movie. It intrigued me, so I decided to purchase a copy and watch it when I returned home. Little did I know; this local director had a gift to create faith-based movies.

The movie opens showing flashbacks of what the family went through while being homeless. Then there is a church scene. As Darrius starts to reminisce about being in church and what church meant to him and how it encouraged him, it's offering time and a minister comes to the congregation to ask the men to give $500. Darrius looks at his wife and his wife looks at him as if to say, "I know 'we' don't have $500 to give. "Immediately, the ushers begin passing the offering plate. Darrius opens up his wallet and sees only a small bill. He begins to put the bill on the offering plate but his wife stops him, as if to say, "That's all the money we have." Darrius shakes his head to say, "I have to give it." Reluctantly, he puts the money in the tray because he knows his wife is not in agreement with what he's doing, but he does it anyway. Then they continue in the service with another praise and worship song: "It's another day's journey and I'm glad about it." The congregation is fully engaged in praising God.

Darrius is sitting next to the grandmother who actually raised him. Unfortunately, she didn't know that they had money struggles and were living on the street. Darrius gave all the money they had. But upon leaving the church, the pastor again reminds him the men are asked to give $500. Darrius is trying to rush away from the church. Meanwhile, his grandmother implies that the men "ought" to be asked for more money. Darrius is uncomfortable, so he tries to pull her away from the church.

Without giving the entire story line away, I want you to watch it for yourself and see if you see yourself in his situation. He was desperate! Darrius didn't have the money. His wife didn't have the money, they didn't have the money. They had little to no money and began to sleep in the car, on the street. The family looked forward to church on Sunday, but most importantly, they looked forward to the fellowship afterwards at the grandmother's house period. She cooked a huge soul food meal, and when you're homeless on the street and you've just given your last in the offering plate and you've been asked to give another $500 that you do not have, every little thing that you can grab a hold to as encouragement you do. So, they love Sunday for the fellowship and the food that they were about to receive as nourishment for their body.

Grandmother could overhear some of the conversation, so she knew that there was an issue—she just didn't know what. Darrius was good at hiding things, but eventually his wife let it slip out that they had a problem. They had a serious problem because he had lost his job! At that moment in his life it was hard for him to be a man. It was hard for his wife to be a wife. People that they trusted and their children saw them go from having things to not having anything. Have you ever been displaced or in despair?

I have. I felt embarrassed and lost. I had too much pride to ask my family for assistance. Plus, I had a full-time job like Darrius.

They ended up at a homeless park where other families were displaced. They shared food, they shared different items and they kept watch over each other to make sure they were safe in the park. One night someone tried to kidnap the girls and the car. Things like this happen all the time depending on the circumstances and the surroundings in the homeless surroundings period. All Darrius had was **prayer**. His pride wouldn't allow him at the time to share with his grandmother what was taking place and him losing his job.

They suffered day in and day out—living in the car, sleeping on the street, and eating outdated food others didn't want. His wife kept reminding him, "Let's do it God's way…let's do it God's way. We have to tell granny, we have to tell your mother [his grandmother] our situation so she can help." But pride wouldn't allow him. As the story continued, they just began to **pray**. They continued to **pray** and they continued to **pray** until something happened. Have you ever lost your job? Have you ever been homeless? Have you ever had any type of lack? Have you ever been presented with an opportunity to pray and you didn't? You thought you had control of the situation; you thought that everything was fine. You were trying to convince yourself, but actually you were in denial. It is in those precious moments that God wants you to speak to him. He wants to hear your voice, whether you are on your job, whether you're having trouble in your marriage, whether you're having problems with your children, and whether you have situations in your neighborhood. God wants to hear from you.

Darrius found out that eventually he had to cry out to God for help, and it was in that cry that he finally started getting vouchers from a teacher at the school and help from his grandmother to get back on their feet. But we have to get past our **pride** and understand that pride and prayer don't go together. Pride and prayer do not go together. So, whenever you have an opportunity to pray for yourself or someone else, use that time. Take advantage of that opportunity to pray. Pray without ceasing. Another translation says, "Keep praying." Keep praying. Don't stop. Keep praying. Keep pressing. Don't stop—whether you are an entrepreneur, leader, Kingdompreneur, millionaire, billionaire—one powerful strategy that a lot of people will not share with you happens to be one that is hidden in plain sight. Just like this movie. The title is Hidden in Plain Sight because what Darrius needed was right before him all the time. What was right before him was everything that had been instilled in him as a youth.

If you remember, when the movie opened he was in church praising God. He had already lost his job and felt a loss, void or something missing in his life that he needed to seek God for. We want to only call on God when it's convenient for us. We only want to call on God when we need something. And we have got to stop that! It is not a strategy of the Word of God to only call on God when you are in need. That is a man-made principle. That has to stop! Rise, Pray and Slay is a biblical principle that's in the Word of God that helps you understand. The Bible says that they rose early in the morning, they prayed, they sought Him, or they came to Him.

So, the same principle, same strategy in the Word of God can be applied today. But we need to read the Word of God. Study the word of God. Live the word of God. And believe the Word of God. No if's, and's or but's. Darrius found out that all he needed was to remember what his grandmother and other saints of God had instilled in him as a youth—prayer. While there are some denominations or religions that are trying to take prayer out of everything, Rise, Pray and Slay is here to put prayer back in everything. So, in all things, pray in all things, give God the glory and if you are a Kingdompreneur, one of the powerful tools you can utilize is prayer and fasting.

Some things come with prayer and fasting. Whether you pray or you pray and fast, there is a divine reason for this action, this experience, this encounter with God so that you can hear him more clearly. Fasting purges and cleanses you of toxins and a lot of unnecessary stuff so that you can hear God more clearly. And it was in those moments when Darrius decided to go back to what he knew and what was instilled in him by praying. He finally felt some relief and God started opening up doors once he got rid of the pride and the other things that was holding him back. And, you have to do the same thing, You have to let go of all of those things that have been holding you back in life, such as your business and career. Let God be God in your business. Let God be God in your families. Let God be

God in everything that you do. And it all goes back to the principle of Rise, Pray and Slay.

See, Darrius thought, that he was losing the respect of his family. He thought that God was punishing him by taking his job, allowing them to sleep in their car, eat in their car, and live out of their car for a period of time. Unbeknownst to him, it was all tied to his pride. They could have long been living a better life after he lost his job but because he had a spirit of pride and he stopped praying, he was overcome with these circumstances. But he had a praying wife that continued to pray and seek God to help her husband and their family, and God did help them. Once Darrius let go of that pride and began to pray, heaven opened up and opportunities were released to them. And, the same thing needs to happen to the spirit of pride cast over this land.

Take a moment to reflect on my accounts of the movie. Did you see yourself in any of these reflections? If so, journal your thoughts. Yes, your notes are personal development areas that may require your attention.

CHAPTER 5

Manage Your Anger...
Don't Let it Manage You!

By Selena Dirden-Ware

I spent a great deal of my life being angry, feeling misunderstood, making up narratives in my head, and not understanding why people seemed not to feel guilt when they hurt me. The Bible says, "Hatred stirs up conflict, but love covers all wrongs" (Proverbs 10:12). Sometimes the people that have hurt you or you feel have wronged you don't even know what they have done, and even if they did hurt you, they may not even care as much as you do. This means you are literally carrying around dead weight.

I had to acknowledge how the smallest things put

me into a fever pitch of anger, how often I would sit in my car and scream, and how I would hit the wall with my bear hand and sprain my wrist in the process. I had to incorporate prayer in my life so that Satan would not take my mind. DAILY PRAYER was the game changer. "I am persuaded that neither death, nor life, neither angels, nor principalities, nor powers, nor things present, nor things to come, nor height, not any other created thing shall be able to separate us from the love of God which is in Christ Jesus our Lord," (Romans 8:38-39).

The results of these daily prayers became my personal superpower and my daily affirmation. This helped subside my anger even in the middle of my anger. Daily prayer also forced me to be more self-aware and be more accountable. Whatever pain, discourse or vengeance you believe that you can cause someone out of retaliation is nothing in comparison to the Lord's vengeance. The Lord's response is based on fact rather than feeling. As you get closer to God's word and you allow Him to change your heart, then you will soon understand that all your help and strength comes from the Lord and he will fight all of your battles. Proverbs 15:1 says, "A soft answer turns away wrath, but a harsh word stirs up anger." You belong to GOD and we need to act like it and help others understand that as well. You have the answers at your fingertips and the only thing you have to do is apply it to your daily walk.

Co-author reflection on the <u>scripture</u>:
"The scripture encouraged me because it made me aware that<u> I could control my response</u>. I was displeasing God by

Romans 8:37-39
New International Version (NIV)

"No, in all these things we are more than conquerors through him who loved us. For I am convinced that neither death nor life, neither angels nor demons, neither the present nor the future, nor any powers, neither height nor depth, nor anything else in all creation, ..."

reacting to situations that did not require a response. If you know God, act like it."

-Selena Dirden-Ware

Phenomenal Prayer Strategy:

Your response dictates your outcome when you ACTIVATE self-control.

It is time to Rise, Pray & Slay!

Manage Your Anger Exercise

When anger festers internally, it opens the door to sickness, unhealthy communication, unhealthy relationships, and other things. Annotate any unresolved anger issues, past or present, that you are ready to let go.

1.

_____

2.

_____

3.

_____

4.

_____

5.

_____

6.

_____

7.

_____

8.

_____

9.

_____

10.

_____

Lord, expose and bind-up all anger in my life!

SAMPLE PRAYER

Prayer time: _____ AM or _____ PM

Prayer day(s): _____

Letting Go of Bitterness

"Father, life seems so unjust, so unfair. The pain of rejection is almost more than I can bear. My past relationships have ended in strife, anger, rejection and separation.

Lord, help me not to be bitter, angry or mad. Help me not to shout or say things to hurt others.

You are the One who has come to free those who have been treated unfairly. I receive emotional healing by faith, and I thank You for giving me the grace to stand firm until the process is complete.

Thank You for wise counselors. Thank You for Your Holy Spirit, my Counselor, who comes to show me what is true. Thank You for helping me to work out with fear and trembling what it really means to be saved. You are working in me, creating in my heart the desire and power to do what pleases You.

In the name of Jesus, I forgive those who have wronged me. I choose to live a life of forgiveness because You have forgiven me. With the help of the Holy Spirit, I rid myself of all bitterness, rage, anger, harsh words, and slander. Flood my heart with kindness that I might be tenderhearted and forgiving. With the help of the Holy Spirit, I will work toward living in peace with everyone and living a holy life. I purpose to protect others so that no one fails to receive the grace of God. I will watch out that no poisonous root of bitterness grows up to trouble me.

I will watch and pray that I don't enter into temptation or cause others to stumble.

Thank You, Father, that those whom the Son makes free and truly free. I have defeated bitterness and resentment by the blood of the Lamb and Your message, in Jesus name, amen."[5]

Now that you have prayed prayers, "Beginning Each Day, Victory Over Depression, Overcoming Feeling of Abandonment, and Letting Go of Bitterness" understand you have the right to Rise, Pray & Slay wherever you go. The issue of separation of church and state has already been determined. Nevertheless, it is up to you to EXERCISE your rights and not be intimidated by your boss, management, atheist, other denominations, etc. when it comes to a prayer regimen. For us to heal the land we must:

(1) Humble ourselves.

(2) Pray.

(3) Seek God's face. Then He will heal the Land. Our world is sick because we lack maturity in these three areas.

Let me ask you some questions:

(1) How humble are you?

(2) Do you only pray when you need something from God?

(3) When is the last time you laid prostrate to seek Him regarding matters of concern?

If your response isn't positive, you can change all of that today as you learn strategies to Rise, Pray & Slay.

CHAPTER 6

Pray Without Ceasing

By Jackie Daniels

A life without prayer is like wondering in the wilderness; just as faith without works is dead. Since I was a child, I've been taught to pray and call Jesus. I'm grateful for that because it helped me through many situations. I couldn't imagine living without God. Steps I take daily in my prayer life begin with being thankful and grateful for God's faithfulness. And lastly, I encourage others. I've learned that we must understand a few things about prayer before we implement it. First, when you are summoning God in prayer for answers, you must be prepared to accept whatever answer He gives you, trust and know that God knows what's best for you, and know that God doesn't want you in pain.

It was a seriously difficult time in my life, when I realized my marriage was at the finish line. I've prayed for years for God to fix it, fix me, fix him. God had showed me many times to let go, but I kept fighting, thinking, "I have to obey the Bible." I followed the scriptures and instructions until God spoke to me. He reminded me of a prayer I prayed asking Him for a certain protection. For me to have this protection I would have to let go and let God handle it. He showed me that I had done my part and that the rest was for Him to work out. Understanding these things would've saved me some trials and tribulations. God has helped me through it all. He has shown me mercy for my disobedience and his grace has given me peace. When I accepted his answer, I was introduced to a peace that was beyond understanding. I know now what unspeakable joy is. We have to believe what we read in the Word of God. We have to stand on His word and promises.

In addition to praying, fasting is required to hear

clearly from God. Fasting is necessary for clarity. When I started fasting, I began to hear God clearly. I could see His word being manifested in my situations. I also lost a little weight in the process! After a seven day fast, on the eighth day, it was finished! I woke up to freedom and peace like I had never known before. My son said, "Mom the heavy weight is gone!" Afterwards, I realized I wasn't fearful of making someone mad, walking around on eggshells or fearing not being happy that day.

My prayer is that people would surrender to God. Allow Him to open up your understanding and channels of forgiveness. You don't have to hold on to fear, anger, grudges, and unforgiveness. Sometimes you don't know you're in bondage until you've been set free.

Co-author reflection on the scripture:

"I wake up praying and I whisper prayers all day. Prayers give me strength and confidence no matter no what is going on."

-Jackie Daniels

Phenomenal Prayer Strategy:

A. Rise early.

B. Spend time in God's presence.

C. Repeat the process to slay things.

1 Thessalonians 5:17
New International Version
(NIV)

"pray continually,"

It is time to Rise, Pray & Slay!

Pray Without Ceasing Exercise

An active prayer life is essential in the life of a believer. Annotate specific things about your job, home or business and which need prayer.

1.
_____

2.
_____

3.
_____

4.
_____

5.
_____

6.
_____

7.
_____

8.
_____

9.
_____

10.
_____

Lord, hear my heart regarding these issues. Teach me strategies to incorporate prayer and fasting!

SAMPLE PRAYER

Prayer time: _____ AM or _____ PM

Prayer day(s): _____

Prayer and Fasting

> "You've commanded, rebuked, prayed prayers, done warfare and shouted, but there's more that needs to be broken off your life. It's time to add some fasting to your warfare strategy. There is no other way around some demonic strongholds."[4]

"Fasting is beneficial whether you fast, partially, or fully. One day fast on a consistent basis will strengthen your spirit over time and give you the ability to disciple yourself for longer fast. Three day fast with just water are a powerful way to see breakthroughs. Esther and the people of Israel went into a three day fast when they were seeking deliverance from death at the hand of Hayman; the king's the king's evil adviser (Esther four and 16). Fast longer than three days should be done by people with more experience in fasting."[4]

30 Strategies for Prayer and Fasting

- Break every chain.

- Fasting destroys stubborn demons and strongholds.

- Fasting increases your strength.

- Fast to overcome the spirit of fear.

- Fast to overcome unbelief and doubt.

- Fast to break the spirit of poverty.

- Fast to break the cycles of failure and defeat.

- Fast to break spirits of procrastination, passivity and slothfulness.

- Fast for healing from infirmity.

- Fast to break free from bitterness, anger and unforgiveness.

- Fast to break free from anxiety and depression.

- Fast to break free from guilt.

- Fast to break free from a painful past.

- Fast to break free from drug and alcohol addiction.

- Fast to break free from gluttony and over indulgence.
- Fast to hear and receive a word from the Lord.
- Fast for deliverance from sexual impurity.
- Fast to break generational curses.
- Fast to break the power of witchcraft, mind control, and ungodly soul ties.
- Fast to break the power of a religious spirit.
- Fast to break the spirit of carnality and double mindedness.
- Fast to break the spirit of pride.
- Fast to break chronic cycles of backsliding.
- Fast for a breakthrough in marriage.
- Fast to restore what's been lost.
- Fast for a breakthrough in the lives of your children.
- Fast to see salvation come to unsaved, loved ones.
- Fast to break the strong holds in your city and nation.
- Fast for the anointing on your life.

- Fast for maintaining breakthrough and deliverance.[4]

Prayers that Close Breaches and Hedges

I close up any breach in my life that would give Satan and demons access, in the name of Jesus (*Ecclesiastics 10:8*).

I pray for every broken hedge in my life to be restored, in the name of Jesus (*Ecclesiastics 10:8*).

I stand in the gap and make up. I stand in the gap and make up the hedge (*Ezekiel 22: 30*).

I repent and receive forgiveness from any sin that has opened the door for any spirit to enter and operate in my life (*Ephesians 4: 27*).

I am a rebuilder of the wall and a repairer of the breach (*Isaiah 58:12*).

I renounce all crooked speech that would cause a breach in the name of Jesus (*Proverbs 15:4*).

Mine of all my breaches, oh Lord (*Isaiah 30:26*).

Let every breach be stopped in the name of Jesus (*Nehemiah 4:7*).

Let my walls be salvation and my gates praise (*Isaiah 60:18*).

I pray for a hedge of protection around my mind, body, finances, possessions and family, in Jesus name.[4]

It is time to Rise, Pray & Slay!

CHAPTER 7

Engulf Yourself in Worship

By Patrice May

I never thought the hymn written by James Rowe in 1912 would be an anthem for my life story. In fact, as a child growing up in church to hear this song the words meant absolutely nothing to me. The writer titled the hymn "Love Lifted Me" and was inspired by Matthew 14:29, when Peter says, "Jesus if it is you, bid me to come." I, too, like Peter was being drawn to come out of a comfortable place and trust the voice of God. I was bold with little to no fear at all. I did not recognize the call of God on my life, and I was in charge of myself and God's plan was the furthest thing from my mind.

My life was my life to live until I faced the heartache of divorce, the death of a child, and the rejection of people. These life events caused me to cry out and surrender my will to God's will. I knew I needed a healer, a savior, and most importantly, the power of God to restore me. I became desperate for Jesus, and my tears were uncontrollable because my heart was broken and full of pain. There was no other place for me to go but to God in prayer.

The presence of God engulfed me, taking my breath away and filling me with a supernatural love to accept myself and forgive others. The Lord met me in prayer and taught me that no matter how painful the disappointment, I had to trust Him with all my heart and not lean on my own understanding (Proverbs 3:5). To trust God was not an easy thing to do, but I wanted to be healed and restored, and without a doubt there is truly restoration in the power of prayer.

Co-author reflection
on the scripture:

My prayer life has taught me how to

have an intimate conversation with God, which is

also known as worship. For it is in worship where I found my worth and the Christ confidence to **RISE** up from every disappointment and to **PRAY** in faith to **SLAY** in grace to walk out God's plan for my life.

Phenomenal Prayer Strategy:

A. Develop an inner worship of an outward expression with God.

B. Understand your worth.

C. Allow a Rise, Pray & Slay regimen to dominate your life.

Jude 24-25
King James Version (KJV)

"Now unto him that is able to keep you from falling, and to present you faultless before the presence of his glory with exceeding joy, to the only wise God our Saviour, be glory and majesty, dominion and power, both now and ever. Amen."

Engulf Yourself in Worship Exercise

SET the atmosphere for worship on your job or wherever you go. List places on your job where you can create a secret place to pray or worship.

1. _____

2. _____

3. _____

4. _____

5. _____

6. _____

7. _____

8. _____

9. _____

10. _____

Lord, remove all my excuses tied to "separation between church and state" so I can come back to you!

SAMPLE PRAYER

Prayer time: _____ AM or _____ PM

Prayer day(s): _____

American Government

"Father, in the name of Jesus, I come to You with a heart of love and concern for America. I intercede for the President of the United States, his cabinet and administration, for all the men and women who serve in Congress, and for our military leaders in the Pentagon. With the help of the Holy Spirit, I bring my requests, prayers and petitions to You and give thanksgiving for all people. I ask that You pour out Your Spirit upon everyone who is in authority in our nation and make Your Word known to them in order that the citizens of this great nation might live a quiet and peaceful life in complete godliness and dignity.

In agreement with Your will, I present my petition on behalf of all who are in authority—our president and all government officials—that they accept Your words and turn their ears toward wisdom, and stretch their minds toward understanding. When they call out for insight and cry aloud for understanding, they will understand the fear of the Lord and discover the knowledge of God. I ask You, Lord, to give our president and his advisors wisdom, knowledge and understanding. I believe that they will understand righteousness and justice as well as integrity. The president's heart is like a stream of water in Your hand, my Lord, and You direct it where You want.

In a multitude of counselors there is safety, and I ask You to give to our president advisors who uphold the ways of righteousness. Give our president and his administration discretion that guards their hearts; give them understanding that protects them and wisdom that rescues them from the evil path of those who twist their words;..."[5]

It is time to Rise, Pray & Slay!

CHAPTER 8

From Fear to Faith

By Angela Kinnel

Back in 2003, while volunteering in a nursing home, I was approached by a minister.

She looked at me and told me that I was going to preach the word of God. I smiled and said, "Oh ok." But in my mind I was like, "Uh-uh, no ma'am!" Looking back at that time in my life, I was saved but still didn't know Jesus or myself. I only knew about Him. I never thought again about the day I was approached. Fast forward to 2006, I was an educator and a member of a church that taught the word of God with simplicity and understanding. While sitting on my bed one day, I had a vision of myself on a stage speaking before a multitude of people. I wondered what it meant. Before I could ask God about it, He told me that I was going to preach His word. I began to weep and ask Him why. I told God that I liked my life and that I didn't want to speak to people. Oddly, I never thought about it again after that day.

Over the years, I was continually experiencing failed relationships, going through a deep depression, questioning my purpose, and having to say goodbye to loved ones because they'd transitioned. I prayed to God for strength because I recognized that I had fallen into a dark place. When you're in that dark place, it's like your life is at a standstill and it takes all you have to get up every day and live. I never forgot that God's word was food for the spirit, so I read and meditated on scriptures like Psalms 23 and 91 to help me fight through the emotional rollercoaster that I was on. Putting up this façade of stability was exhausting and made me feel worse. I got tired and finally surrendered to God. I knew that if I was going to get better, I had to rely on Him only. Immediately after I surrendered, God reminded me of what I'd been told back in 2003 and 2006. I'd completely forgotten about both moments. I realized that I'd been running in fear all along from the purpose of my existence.

I rededicated my life to the Lord and established a life of prayer. I didn't want to waste any more time so I entered seminary for two years and never looked back. However, it wasn't without fear of what my family and friends would say about me. There were those who were very supportive and those who seemed very skeptic. I must admit that I had doubts of whether I was truly called to minister the word of God. It wasn't until I began to learn and understand my identity in Jesus Christ that I was able to see myself as He did and embrace His will for my life.

Co-author reflection on the scripture:

"They gave me peace and the confidence I needed to walk in my calling."

-Angela Kinnel

Phenomenal Prayer Strategy:

A. Receive salvation and get to know Jesus.

B. Come into the knowledge of Christ for yourself.

C. Receive the vision or mission he gives you, even if you do not understand it.

D. Begin to read and meditate on God's word.

E. Establish a **prayer life**.

Deuteronomy 31:6
Amplified (AMP)

"Be strong, courageous, and firm; fear not nor be in terror before them, for it is the Lord your God who goes with you; He will not fail you or forsake you."

It is time to Rise, Pray & Slay!

From Fear to Faith Exercise

What is hindering you from accepting the call God has on your life or what do you fear? List these items and call them out in your prayer time.

1. _____

2. _____

3. _____

4. _____

5. _____

6. _____

7. _____

8. _____

9. _____

10. _____

Lord, I know fear does not come from you. Please remove the seed of fear and allow me to walk in faith.

Sustainability Prayer Tools

New King James Version (NKJV)
Source: BibleGateway.com

There are times when people become discourage about praying like Darrius due to the lack of a sustainability plan. Here are a few for you. First, humble yourself. Next, identify the prayer strategy in each scripture. Lastly, apply it to your Rise, Pray & Slay regimen. We know your life will never be the same.

Matthew 6:9
The Model Prayer

In this manner, therefore, pray:

Our Father in heaven,
Hallowed be Your name.
Your kingdom come.
Your will be done
On earth as *it is* in heaven.
Give us this day our daily bread.
And forgive us our debts,
As we forgive our debtors.
And do not lead us into temptation,

But deliver us from the evil one.
For Yours is the kingdom and the power and the glory forever. Amen.

2 Samuel 21:14
They buried the bones of Saul and Jonathan his son in the country of Benjamin in Zelah, in the tomb of Kish his father. So, they performed all that the king commanded. And after that God heeded the **prayer** for the land.

1 Kings 8:22
Solomon's Prayer of Dedication
Then Solomon stood before the altar of the LORD in the presence of all the assembly of Israel, and spread out his hands toward heaven;

1 Kings 8:28-29
Yet regard the **prayer** of Your servant and his supplication, O Lord my God, and listen to the cry and the **prayer** which <u>Your</u> <u>servant</u> is praying before You today: that Your <u>eyes</u> <u>may</u> <u>be</u> <u>open</u> toward this temple night and day, toward the place of which You said, 'My name shall be there,' that You may hear the **prayer** which Your servant makes toward this place.

2 Kings 19:4
It may be that the Lord your God will hear all the words of *the* Rabshakeh, whom his master the king of Assyria

has sent to reproach the living God, and will rebuke the words which the Lord your God has heard. Therefore lift up *your* **prayer** for the <u>remnant</u> that is left.'"

Ezra 8:21-23
Fasting and Prayer for Protection

Then I proclaimed a fast there at the river of Ahava, that we might <u>humble</u> <u>ourselves</u> before our God, to seek from Him the <u>right</u> <u>way</u> for us and our little ones and all our possessions. For I was ashamed to request of the king an escort of soldiers and horsemen to help us against the enemy on the road, because we had spoken to the king, saying, "The hand of our God *is* upon all those <u>for good</u> <u>who</u> <u>seek</u> <u>Him</u>, but His power and His wrath *are* against all those who forsake Him." So we fasted and entreated our God for this, and He answered our **prayer**.

Psalm 7:1
[**Prayer** *and Praise for Deliverance from Enemies*] [*A Meditation of David, which he sang to the Lord concerning the words of Cush, a Benjamite.*] O Lord my God, in You I put my trust; <u>Save</u> <u>me</u> from all those who <u>persecute</u> <u>me</u>; And <u>deliver</u> <u>me</u>,

Psalm 9:1

[**Prayer** and Praise for Deliverance from Enemies] [A Meditation of David, which he sang to the Lord concerning the words of Cush, a Benjamite.] O Lord my God, in You I put my trust; Save me from all those who persecute me; And deliver me,

Psalm 28:1
[Rejoicing in Answered **Prayer**] [A Psalm of David.] To You I will cry, O Lord my Rock: Do not be silent to me, Lest, if You are silent to me, I become like those who go down to the pit.

Psalm 30:1
[The Blessedness of Answered **Prayer**] [A Psalm. A Song at the dedication of the house of David.] I will extol You, O Lord, for You have lifted me up, And have not let my foes rejoice over me.

Psalm 39:1
[**Prayer** for Wisdom and Forgiveness] [To the Chief Musician. To Jeduthun. A Psalm of David.] I said, "I will guard my ways, Lest I sin with my tongue; I will restrain my mouth with a muzzle, While the wicked are before me."

Psalm 43:1

[**Prayer** *to God in Time of Trouble*] <u>Vindicate</u> <u>me</u>, O God, And <u>plead</u> <u>my</u> <u>cause</u> against an ungodly nation; Oh, deliver me from the deceitful and unjust man!

Psalm 51:1

[*A* **Prayer** *of Repentance*] [*To the Chief Musician. A Psalm of David when Nathan the prophet went to him, after he had gone in to Bathsheba.*] <u>Have</u> <u>mercy</u> <u>upon</u> <u>me</u>, O God, According to Your lovingkindness; According to the multitude of Your tender mercies, <u>Blot</u> <u>out</u> <u>my</u> <u>transgressions</u>.

Psalm 54:1

[*Answered* **Prayer** *for Deliverance from Adversaries*] [*To the Chief Musician. With* <u>*stringed*</u> <u>*instruments*</u>. *A Contemplation of David when the Ziphites went and said to Saul, "Is David not hiding with us?"*] Save me, O God, by Your name, And vindicate me by Your strength.

1 Samuel 2:1-3
Hannah's Prayer
And Hannah prayed and said:

<u>My</u> <u>heart</u> <u>rejoices</u> in the LORD;
<u>My</u> <u>horn</u> is <u>exalted</u> in the LORD.

I smile at my enemies,
Because I rejoice in Your salvation.

"No one is holy like the LORD,
For *there is* none besides You,
Nor *is there* any rock like our God.

"Talk no more so very proudly;
Let no arrogance come from your mouth,
For the LORD *is* the God of knowledge;
And by Him actions are weighed.

Psalm 69:13

But as for me, my **prayer** *is* to You, O Lord, *in* the acceptable time; O God, in the multitude of Your mercy, Hear me in the truth of Your salvation.

Psalm 83:1

[**Prayer** *to Frustrate Conspiracy Against Israel*] [*A Song. A Psalm of Asaph.*] Do not keep silent, O God! Do not hold Your peace, And do not be still, O God!

Psalm 85:1

[**Prayer** *that the Lord Will Restore Favor to the Land*] [*To the Chief Musician. A Psalm of the sons of Korah.*] Lord, You have been favorable to Your land; You have brought back the captivity of Jacob.

Psalm 86:1
[**Prayer** *for Mercy, with Meditation on the Excellencies of the Lord*] [*A* **Prayer** *of David.*] Bow down Your ear, O Lord, hear me; For I *am* poor and needy.

Psalm 90:1
[*BOOK FOUR*] [*Psalms 90–106*] [*The Eternity of God, and Man's Frailty*] [*A* **Prayer** *of Moses the man of God.*] Lord, You have been our dwelling place in all generations.

Mark 11:25
[*Forgiveness and* **Prayer**] "And whenever you stand praying, if you have anything against anyone, forgive him, that your Father in heaven may also forgive you your trespasses.

Please allow us to recommend some reference tools to assist you through your transformation.

It is time to Rise, Pray & Slay!

Tools and Reference Notes

1. Goll, James W., The Lost Art of Intercession: Restoring the Power and Passion of the Watch of the Lord, p. 44. Florida, Charisma House, 2016.
2. The First Amendment (Amendment 1), United States Constitution, It was adopted on Dec. 15, 1791, as one of the ten amendments that constitute the Bill of Rights, Wikipedia.
3. Brow, Michael, Prayer Never Fails, Insider, Pureflix.com, Lifestyle movie channel, Director Wes Miller, 2016.
4. Eckhardt, John, Fasting for Breakthrough & Deliverance, p. v, 1, 4, 135.
5. Copeland, Germaine, Prayers that avail much, (Gold Letter Edition), p.43, 87, 132,133, 154, 157, 205, 343-344.
6. Jefferson, Thomas. Jefferson's Letter to the Danbury Baptists: The Final Letter, as Sent. The Library of Congress Information Bulletin: June 1998, Lib. of Cong., June 1998, Web. Aug 7, 2010, Wikipedia.
7. Prayer Power Tools, New King James Version (NKJV), Source: BibleGateway.com.
8. Lee, Linda D., In Bed with a Snake, p. 135-136, Dallas-Fort Worth, LL Media Group, LLC, 2010, 2016.

Names of God

1) Jehovah Jireh   Provider

2) Jehovah Nissi   Banner

3) Jehovah Shalom   Peace

4) Jehovah Rohi   Shepherd

5) Jehovah Tsidkenu   Righteousness

6) Jehovah Rapha   Healer

7) Jehovah Shammah   Present

8) El Shaddai   All Mighty

9) Jehovah Mekaddishkem   Sanctifier

10) Jehovah Adonai   Sovereign

11) El Gibbar   Mighty God

12) Jehovah Sabaoth   Warrior

13) YHWH   I Am

14) El Elyon   The God Most High

They took prayer out of "EVERYTHING." Now use the names of God to put Him back in everything!

We hope you have been enriched and encouraged by the stories of these phenomenal overcomers and divine prayer strategies. We would like to challenge you!

Call-to-action:

THEY TOOK PRAYER OUT OF "EVERYTHING."

AND WE NEED YOUR HELP TO PUT IT BACK IN EVERYTHING!

Please share ways you will **implement** the strategies learned in this book to shift your workplace culture, global situation(s), and increase your prayer life.

1.

2.

3.

4.

As stated in the beginning, you have a "natural right to pray." But also, you have a "spiritual right to pray." Use both to help <u>heal</u> <u>the</u> <u>land</u>!

Meet the Authors

Visionary **Linda D. Lee** is the CEO and Founder of LL Media Group, LLC, a Personal Development Consultancy company. She is a Professional Certified Life Coach (PCLC), Certified Christian Mentor (CCM), International Speaker, Personal Development Consultant, Award-winning author, and a voice for the voiceless. She has amassed over 20 years' combined experience in personal development, customer service, and Emotion Management Strategies.

Professionally, she is a two-time recipient of Former President Obama Gold and Bronze Volunteer Service Award, Dallas-Ft. Worth Federal Executive Board Public Service Excellence Recognition Award, Human Capital & Training Coaching Ambassador Pilot Program, and two-time graduate of Glynco Law Enforcement Academy. Linda is a Graduate of Rockhurst University

Business Programmed Course and numerous other accolades.

With her years of experience and wealth of revelatory knowledge, she touches lives through workshops and webinars to build healthy relationships virtually or physically, as a *Family Relationship Midwife,* ® one mindset at a time.

As a prolific writer, she has been labeled a 'Powerhouse Phenomenon' by Huffington Post. Her creditability has been established on the international syndicated platforms STARR Radio UK, KHVN Heaven 97, The Cedric Bailey Show, LaVida News, Immerss TV, I Am Princess of Suburbia TV, *I Am A Storyteller Magazine, Queen "B" Magazine*, Access 34 TV, Anthony Chisom Conversations TV Show, The Ricardo Miller Show, Fishbowl Radio Network, Stellar Award Candidate 'Big Mouth' Radio Show, *Modern Citizen Magazine, Today's Purpose Woman Magazine, YOU Magazine, Divine Inspiration Magazine,* and others. Linda is the author of, *In Bed with a Snake, How to Divorce a Curse, FREEDOM: Creating a Therapeutic Culture of Men, and Lifting the Veil: Transitioning from a Ministry to Business Mindset. In Bed with a Snake* was the winner of the Black Essence Inc. "Excellent Book" Award and the 2018 Indie Author Legacy finalist for Memoir of the Year.

Linda garnered respect and admiration as she facilitated workshops and undertook speaking engagements in Cape Coast, Ghana, Africa, and London, UK. In 2018, she facilitated the Man-Up Summit to restore the voice of men and remove the stigma regarding their communication, counseling and trauma. Additionally, she launched the inaugural Tutor Purity Ceremony to teach others how to have healthy relationships and live a life pleasing to God. In the near future, she will launch global Purity Workshops in Mozambique, Africa and Johannesburg, South Africa with Mozambique Ambassador, Dr. Lindie Sanders.

Linda and her husband, Bruce, live in Dallas-Ft. Worth. They have three children, seven grandchildren and two great-grandchildren. Both are licensed preachers and service the community in multiple capacities. As well, both enjoy facilitating personal development. Bruce specializes in Trauma Informed Care and Linda in building healthy relationships with positive competencies, sustainability plans, and alternative rite of passage ceremonies. She can be reached at www.1lindadlee.com or lintr.ee/1lindadlee.

Dr. Lindie J. Massinga-Sanders is an educator, minister, researcher, businesswoman and philanthropist based in Tucson, Arizona, USA. After teaching in public education for 24 years, she now dedicates her life to spreading the Gospel through ministry of helps training and preaching globally.

She is the ambassador for U.S.-based National Regeneration Fellowship of Christian Churches (NRFoCC) in Southern Africa. When she is home, Dr. Lindie leads the LEAP Intercessory Prayer Team; she is a student at God's Special Forces Unit Ministries (GSFUM), and a member of Overcomers Deliverance and Healing Ministries. Her non-profit organization, *I Can Do All Things, Inc.* (ICDAT), helps local families provide better opportunities to their children.

Additionally, Dr. Massinga-Sanders manages *Global Creations LLC* whose ongoing services include two online businesses. Working alongside two fellow educators, she is currently raising funds to build a state-of-the-art secondary boarding school to serve the community of Boane in Southern Mozambique. She can be reached at globalcreations85712@gmail.com.

It is time to Rise, Pray & Slay!

Angela Tamica Kinnel is a 12-year veteran educator, ordained minister, best-selling author, and public speaker. Her passion is to encourage, motivate and educate the world about Jesus Christ and their identity in Him.

Angela earned a Bachelor of Science degree in Agricultural Economics from Fort Valley State University and went on to pursue a Master of Science degree in the same area at Tuskegee University. She obtained a Master of Arts degree in Education with an emphasis in curriculum and instruction and is also a 2017 graduate of World Changers Bible School where she earned an associate degree in Christian Studies. Angela has co-authored two books: *Identity: Who do you think you are?* and Amazon best-seller, *Soul Talk Volume 2*.

A native of Dawson, Georgia, Angela currently resides in the metro Atlanta area and is a member of World Changers Church International in College Park, Georgia. She can be reached at aktheauthor.net

It is time to Rise, Pray & Slay!

Debbie Humphrey is a Visionary of Ministry through dramatic interpretation and most recent The #GIRLUP movement. She has the support of her husband, Minister James Humphrey, Music and Arts Pastor at Kingdom Life Fellowship Church under the leadership of Pastor Lee and Donna Edwards.

Working in the music and arts, stage and film for several years has prepared Debbie for the ministry God would place in her. She has ministered in churches and conferences throughout North Texas and Oklahoma.

God uses Debbie to minister to people with hurt, pain, loneliness and even depression. Health2Healing

Ministry (H2H) was birthed while she was in many of those dark places and she cried out, "God, heal me where I hurt!"

She currently interns with Braeden Chance Productions and is a part of the Poorchild Films team.

Debbie and her husband James are the proud parents of three handsome young men, LaDerrieus, Anthony and Jarell. She can be reached on her Facebook platform.

It is time to Rise, Pray & Slay!

Sha-Miracle Demus is the CEO of Jazzy Jewels of Christ Women's Ministry. The vision for the ministry was birthed from her testimony of being an OVERCOMER! Her mission is to spiritually equip and empower women globally. The ministry is devoted to fostering authentic sisterhood and encouraging women to radiate the righteousness of Christ.

She is in the process of launching an expansion of the ministry called B.M.O.B. (Bonus Moms of Benevolence - Doing it God's Way). This portion of the ministry aims to spiritually educate, inspire and encourage this particular audience of women as well as serve as a voice for them in their struggle.

She is a wife, bonus mother, author, teacher, worship leader, visionary and evangelist. She resides in Dallas with her loving husband, Frederick Demus and son Darius. She has a heart to serve God's people and can be reached at www.jazzyjewelsofchrist.com or at Jazzyjewelsofchrist@yahoo.co.

It is time to Rise, Pray & Slay!

Selena Ware is a native of Texas. She earned a Bachelor's of Science degree in Computer Information Systems, a certification in Lean Six Sigma Process Improvement and a CompTia Security + certification.

Selena is an Automation Technology Leader at a Fortune 500 company and manages the strategy for a $4M portfolio of work.

Selena is also a retired Navy veteran who served 22 years and received Good Conduct Medals, 2 Navy Achievement Medals and selected for Regional Sailor of the Year.

Her favorite thing to do is spending time with her husband, son and wonderful family.

Regardless of achievements and degrees, Selena has been protected by grace and mercy. Selena grew up in church her entire life but did not truly develop a personal relationship with God until she experienced her own trials and tribulations. God's grace has saved her from life threatening mistakes and bad decisions. She can be reached online through her Facebook platform.

It is time to Rise, Pray & Slay!

Jacquelyn Daniels is a cheerful, loving and powerful woman of God who strives daily to walk in the spirit of love and servitude. Her heart for God's people is contagious and she spreads his love to all of those that she encounters. Minster Daniels is originally from Houston, Texas and is the proud mother of three adult sons. Jacquelyn is the owner of Jackie's Hair Café, a unique hair salon here in the Dallas Fort Worth area where women can come to relax, relate and release. With fifteen years of experience, she has become one of the most creative and talented stylists around.

Jacquelyn was ordained as a licensed minister of the Gospel at Loving Fellowship Church in DeSoto, Texas where she remains faithfully involved. Serving in ministry for over thirty-five years has taught Jackie a wealth of knowledge. She is a woman of God who believes in the power of encouragement. Jacquelyn can be reached online through her Facebook platform.

It is time to Rise, Pray & Slay!

Patrice May is a Bachelors of Arts graduate from Southern University, Baton Rouge Louisiana and a Masters of Arts graduate from Amberton University in Garland Texas, Doctoral Degree candidate in Education and a licensed minster since 2013. Patrice was born in Milwaukee Wisconsin but now resides in Dallas, Texas.

She is a gifted 21st century visionary, an education enthusiast, and the Founder Executive Director of InSpire, a premier nonprofit organization which provides wraparound and enrichment programming for children and families. The agency has a proven record of improved test scores, increased positive behaviors and exposure to creative learning opportunities for its participants. Because of the impactful programs InSpire has been able to secure program grants and private funds to exceed $100,000.00.

Patrice is a prolific motivational speaker that has spoken all across the country. You can connect with her at www.inspirealife2.com.

It is time to Rise, Pray & Slay!

www.ingramcontent.com/pod-product-compliance
Lightning Source LLC
Chambersburg PA
CBHW071146090426
42736CB00012B/2244